T0148339

VENETA JUNCTIoN

A Mother's Journey

Dale Willis
Diane Figueiredo
Sharleen Kapp

iUniverse, Inc.
New York   Bloomington

Veneta Junction
A Mother's Journey

Copyright © Sharleen Kapp

iUniverse books may be ordered through booksellers or by contacting:

iUniverse
1663 Liberty Drive
Bloomington, IN 47403
www.iuniverse.com
1-800-Authors (1-800-288-4677)

ISBN: 978-1-4502-2135-1 (pbk)
ISBN: 978-1-4502-2139-9 (cloth)
ISBN: 978-1-4502-2136-8 (ebk)

Printed in the United States of America

iUniverse rev. date: 4/20/2010

CONTENTS

ACKNOWLEDGMENTS

Our thanks go out to Bernice Dorgan for lending us her memory. When we frequently became lost in the intricacies of Veneta's journey she was there with guidelines. Special thanks also to Meta Thornedyke for her many editing suggestions. And Sharleen, especially, sends thanks to Jamie Markus, one of Veneta's great granddaughters, for her generous gift used for the publishing of this book.

INTRODUCTION

We began this writing adventure about a year ago, following Veneta's last birthday gathering of her children. Before that, the concept had begun as a collection of her stories that we had heard from childhood, and her son Dale had compiled. Then we considered adding a memorable incident from each of us. From that point, somehow it morphed into a chronicle of her life journey, with two favorite stories tacked on the end.

We were trying to record a span of only about one hundred and twenty years, give or take a few. In retrospect, it might have been easier to track the migration of Marco Polo across Asia and through the Khyber Pass, since his progress had been more clearly recorded, and there would be no surviving members of his army to cite evidence that would decry any of our conclusions. In this instance, there are people still living from much of the time covered, and offspring of people who had lived earlier, who had to be considered. Some had their own interpretations of when and how things had happened. And in most cases we only had a picture of a gravestone, a couple of death certificates, a few photos with names occasionally written along the edges, and a census report or two that could be used as validation—Veneta's memory not as intact as it was before she passed the century mark.

Nonetheless, we persevered. And in the doing we discovered new depths to our mother. We celebrate her tenacity and gentleness, and are satisfied to leave any residual facts or fancies to others. They may do additional research and ponder the more focused information if they feel inspired to do that.

To readers we offer the softer edges of a lengthy journey, and a peek into who our mother was, and is. We hope that readers, both family and friends, will tolerate and even celebrate the inaccuracies, since these are all memories and subject to the natural erosion that happens when facts are so dependent on one's personal experience. We intend this book to be a tribute to the gentle parenting and magic of our mom.

VENETA'S STORY

Veneta (Ven-ee´-ta) was born in Canada, probably on the farm in Nova Scotia, on April 27th, 1909. It is said that she was born with a veil over her face. Such a rare phenomenon, possibly affecting only one baby in eighty thousand births, was considered by many to be an indication that she would not only be lucky, but she would have second sight such as telepathy or clairvoyance. And, in truth, she often did visualize things in her dreams that later came true, whether they were the result of clairvoyance or intuition or simple intelligent insight.

We do not know much about Veneta's mother's early life. We do know that her name was Annie May and she was the daughter of Elizabeth (Bessie) Manning and Alexander McDonald, information taken from Annie May's death certificate. A 1901 census suggests that she had married young to a man named Graham, and had lived in Massachusetts in the USA for a while. She was twenty-four when she returned alone to the farm and her mother, Bessie, who had married for the second time, to Montagu Robertson. Annie May's new stepfather Montagu, who originally came from Germany, owned acres and acres on two big farms near the mines in McLellan's Brook, Pictou County, Nova Scotia. He rented one farm, and worked the other.

There were two other children, Josie and Hazel, who became part of the family when their mother, a sick cousin, could no longer care for them. She had turned them over to Annie May to raise as her own daughters. Later, when Annie May crossed into the States with Martin, she left the girls on the farm with Bessie and Montagu, where they could grow up as daughters, and help on the farm.

Martin Dupree, Veneta's father, was from New Brunswick, Canada, where his family also had a prosperous farm. Unfortunately, while Martin was still young his parents had been killed in a buggy accident, leaving four teenaged sons, Mike, Walter, Nelson and Martin, and one daughter, Emma.

Mike, the oldest, crossed into the USA in 1903 and eventually established a farm in Peabody, Massachusetts. In 1930 he moved his farm to Brockton, Mass., on land that may have become the site of the Brockton Veterans' Administration. From there he and his wife Lena moved his farm to Bridgewater, Mass., where Lena also worked as a radio interpreter.

Uncle Mike was the uncle who was called Popeye because he looked like that cartoon character. It was also said that he never washed his coffee cup or coffee pot because he felt washing it would take away the flavor.

Veneta's grandmother
Elizabeth Manning Robertson (Bessie)

Bessie and Montagu Robertson

In this picture taken in front of the Robertson house, we see Bessie on a horse, a hired-hand standing watching, and Josie down front with the dog.

Bessie and Montagu memorial in a Cemetery in McLellan's Brook, Pictou County, Nova Scotia.

Mike and Lena had four lovely daughters, Lila, Ada, Beatrice and Marie, and three sons, Fred, Hector and Henry. Their oldest son, Fred, was killed while drinking in Boston, Mass. They believed he was murdered. His father took it particularly hard. He and his son had been at odds much of the time, particularly when his son didn't want to get up in the mornings. "Come on, we need to go to work," he'd say.

"Oh, I'm so tired," his son would complain.

There was always sadness. Once when Veneta visited a married cousin she learned about a son they had lost a short time before. He was ten when he, along with another boy, fell into a hole in a field after they had been told not to play in that spot. Two horses were also killed in that hole. The horses slipped in and tore themselves up trying to get out, but couldn't get any footing even though the hole was in fact only a large puddle of mud made worse by their struggling.

A second Dupree brother, Walter, settled in Haverhill, Massachusetts, where there was work in the shoe factory. His wife, Aunt Agnes, also worked at the shoe factory, and was always wonderful to Veneta when she would visit as a youngster.

Nelson, the third brother, settled somewhere in the Boston area. We learned very little about him other than that he possibly worked as a telephone lineman.

Martin, the youngest Dupree brother, who also wanted to go to the States, worked for a period of time in the McLellan's Brook mines near the Robertson farm, and eventually became a farmhand for the Robertsons. He met Annie May there. They were soon married and remained on the farm for a while. And when he was ready to go across the border, Annie May was ready to go with him.

We believe they stopped for a while in Maine where Martin worked in the coal mines or the logging camps, then moved on to Mike's farm in Peabody where he was certain to get steady work. While they lived in Peabody they had four children, Edgar, born in 1904, Ira, Wallas and Monte soon after. Unfortunately, the younger three died from a serious illness, meningitis or influenza, in 1907 or '08. Edgar was also ill and, though he recovered, the severity of the illness took its toll. It was predicted he would not live beyond forty-five. (Interestingly, he died at forty-eight, not so far off the mark, on a lunch break at Blueberry Farm in Maine.)

Annie May and Martin returned with Edgar to the Robertson farm. They were there for about four years during which they had Veneta, Bill, and Georgie. Then, in 1911, when Veneta was three, the family again crossed into the USA and settled once more in Peabody.

While they were living there, when Veneta was six years old, she was sent to spend some time with a cousin who had settled with her family not too far away. She was not going there to look after a baby or to help with house work. She was going for the summer to temporarily lighten the load on her own mother, who had a number of things to contend with, and was likely due to deliver an additional child during Veneta's summer away. In the fall she would return home.

Though it was a short distance, it was the first time Veneta had gone anywhere alone on a train, an adventure made even more unsettling when she reached her destination at a small depot in the middle of nowhere and there was no attendant or ticket agent. There were no people or houses anywhere in sight. There was just a narrow countryside road that lead off in one direction.

Courageously following her mother's instructions, she picked up her small case and began walking, and soon came to a fork with nothing to indicate which branch she was to take. Just at that moment two crows flew down the road to the right. Veneta had always been fascinated by crows. Her brother Edgar once brought a single crow home, splitting its tongue to teach it to talk, and it seemed like their mother never had any good luck after that. She also remembered the poem her grandmother had taught her that went:

One crow sorrow
Two crows joy
Three crows a letter
Four crows a boy…

Since there were two crows that flew straight down one way, she followed them unafraid. She walked on around a long curve and down a short hill, and there was a little bridge and then a farm with a fruit and vegetable stand out front and a house where her cousin lived, just like her mama told her. And there was her cousin watching for her. She knew everything was going to be fine. The crows had been an indication that the Lord was watching over her. For the rest of her life she remembered that crows were messengers to be considered carefully.

It was following that, when she was back in Peabody with her mother, that Veneta dreamt about their house burning to the ground, leaving only the face of a man staring up at her through the ashes. Unfortunately, the following day the house did burn, along with Veneta's brand new doll and doll carriage inside. While Annie May unsuccessfully tried to stop the fire before it got up the stairway, Veneta struggled to rescue her doll, the only one she had ever owned. She tugged on the carriage in spite of her mother yelling for her to get out of the house.

They were lucky none of them were hurt, because the fire wagon was too big to make it up the narrow road and the house was totally consumed. In the ashes, about all that was recognizable was the remnant of an oatmeal box with the face of the Quaker man on it, the same face Veneta had seen in her dream.

The next thing we know is that they moved to Hanson, Massachusetts shortly after that. Martin had been hired by Hood milk, possibly through his brother Mike's business connections.

The kids were getting older. Edgar learned to play the bugle, for instance, and proudly played Taps on the town hall steps for one holiday celebration. But like most kids, they found all sorts of ways to be difficult. One time, Bill and Georgie lit a fire in the woods, and that could have been disastrous. Their mother spanked their bottoms, because when those two were together they always got in trouble. Georgie, whose full name was actually Georgie Washington Dupree, because she was born on Washington's birthday, was a little Dickens, and Bill just went along with anything.

Veneta, who loved to read and learn, went to school instead of playing. She remembered that there was a crazy man who hung around the school house. He was attracted to the children and frightened them. Once, when he got inside, the teacher let the fire in the stove get high enough to make the school house so hot and uncomfortable he left. But unfortunately, one day he got between the school house and the outhouse where Veneta was. When the teacher thought it was safe she shouted "Run, Veneta, run!" As soon as she got Veneta inside she locked the door, and kept it locked until it was time for them to go home.

They were still in Hanson when Martin got injured on his job as a milkman, and was offered lifetime employment as a result. But since Montagu had given land to Annie May and Martin, they decided to return to the farm in Canada and build a house on a beautiful spot at the top of a hill and settle down. Martin, Annie May and the children, Edgar, Veneta, Bill, Georgie and Bernice, were all together while the house was being built, and everyone was happy.

Bernice has a memory of playing in the snow back then. When they would go in, Annie May would have set a washtub full of warm water in the middle of the kitchen floor so they could stand in it until their cold feet felt thawed.

Veneta's Grandpa Robertson was a very proud man. His hay fields had to be mowed just so and the hay stacked to be stored for the long winters, everything trim and neat. And all the buckets and buildings were cleaned constantly. He never allowed the children to play up near the cows, though he enjoyed watching Veneta running through the fields, her auburn hair flying up and golden in the sun. He told her she was a joy to him.

The dairy produce from the Robertson farm was sold in New Glasgow, Nova Scotia, and other places. Veneta could remember that when she was very young she would watch her Grandmother Bessie load up the wagon for delivery to the markets in the city.

There was a collie, and a bulldog, to take care of the farm. They would protect the cows in the field and round them up when needed. As working dogs they were not for the children's entertainment. But Bill had one smaller dog, Billy Jigs, which Veneta and her sisters and brothers enjoyed. When Veneta would run up the hill, Billy Jigs, who couldn't see very well, would run after her and grab her dress. She thought that was very funny, like playing tag. Then her brother Bill would run down the hill with Billy Jigs, and because the dog's eyes were so bad, he would run into anything in his way, once even a horse. Fortunately, that usually didn't cause injury to the dog and made the children laugh as well. But every once in a while there was a thud when

Robertson's team

Edgar and Wallas, one of Annie May's three young sons who died as babies.

Bill and Billy Jigs, the blind dog.

The Robertson's sitting outside their home.

the dog would run headfirst into an outbuilding, a scary thing to happen even if he was not actually harmed.

Veneta was eventually given a cute collie puppy for her own. At least she thought it was hers. Then one day a woman came who really wanted the pup. Veneta's heart was broken when Annie May gave it to her. Losing that puppy remained a sad memory all of Veneta's life, even after she learned that the real reason was they were getting ready to move again to the States—the place Martin had always intended to settle, near his brothers.

When she wasn't racing through the fields with the dog and her siblings, Veneta was a quiet, innovative child who loved playing house for hours all by herself. She had some little pieces of glass she pretended were her dishes. And occasionally, when no one was watching, she would go into the house to get some real butter to put on a dish. She had to climb up high to where it was stored for everyday use. She also retained memories of the cool cellar where the bulk of the butter was kept. Butter was always a special treat for her. She loved to bite into it and leave her teeth marks in the shiny yellow surface. When she heard they were leaving the farm, Veneta gathered all her little pieces of glass together and tucked them away under the corner of one of the farm buildings so she could find them if she ever came back, which she never did.

During the writing of this, Dale wondered if the building was still there with the bits of glass still under the corner. He could picture going to that farm and finding the house up on the hill all boarded up and untouched since the day Veneta left. She kept the deed and still had it after all that time. He hoped that ownership had eventually reverted back to the Robertsons, who might have taken care of the house from then until now.

Moving children around was not something that parents wanted or liked doing back then. It was just good economics for struggling families. Children were both assets and loved family members. Josie and Hazel, for instance, would help on the farm as well as being considered new daughters. It was a perfect fit.

Eventually Annie May had four daughters, Veneta, Georgie, Bernice and Hazel's child Mona. And she had four sons, Edgar, Bill and Carl, as well as the elusive Jim Kelly who lived with his father, a sea captain. Later on, in the forties, even Edgar's fiancee's son Billy Gibbons was in her care. She moved them around here and there as they were needed, mostly the girls. But during all that time she held the family together. Home was where mama was. It was a workable system of extending and saving families from permanent separation, such as orphanages and adoption.

Working in the mines was a very difficult life. It was understandable that Martin frequently went with the rest of the miners for a drink after work. Regrettably, Annie May occasionally needed to go into town, almost five miles away, to bring him home. One night that Veneta clearly recalled, there was a heavy snow storm, the wind high and the world so covered in drifted snow that she was sure her mother would never make it home again. She had worked herself into a sobbing tizzy by the time her mother got back. Annie May, unable to comfort Veneta, finally told her to stop carrying on and threw her out the door into a snow bank. She remembered that tumbling into the snow bank didn't hurt a bit, but the shock of the cold was enough to stop her hysteria and make her realize her parents were safe and all was well.

Veneta loved her French-speaking papa. He was very proud and very proper. And when he was not working he was always well dressed and handsome. She thought that the black that remained around his eyes even after he washed up was attractive. All the men who worked in the mines had that look. She had no idea that it was indicative of the miserable nature of digging coal.

All miners were superstitious. It was, for instance, believed to be bad luck if a woman was the first person to knock on your door on New Year's Day. And if a miner passed a women on his way to work he would take it as such a bad omen he would turn around and go home. All of that and just the nature of the work convinced Martin that it was time to go back to the States and try again.

For a year or so they were stuck in St. John, New Brunswick, waiting for the opportunity to cross into the States after having been denied until they had the proper papers. It was during that time that Veneta would go with her siblings to watch the water rise or sink in a tide pool there. They would sit on a boat that a fisherman left on the bank and safely watch the whirlpool. Even at that age, seven or eight, she knew not to get too close. When the swirling water went down, she knew if she wasn't careful she could go down with it and be lost forever.

Eventually the city put up fences and installed seats where people could sit safely and watch.

It was also in St. John that a local movie house had a freckle contest. Bill and Veneta, who were like twins, had the most freckles. Bill came in first and Veneta second. She was glad that Bill won because they got money or movie passes and she would have given them to him in either case.

When the family tried to cross into the USA in 1918, only Martin was allowed because of a ring he was wearing that meant he was a member of some organization, possibly the Masons. The ring may have indicated that Martin would be able to get work in the States. Then he could send for the rest of the family and they would be allowed to cross the border as well. In the meantime, Annie May and the children stayed for the school year in St. John, until she received a letter from Martin with pictures that indicated he was settled and had a place for them. Veneta never did get a full year of schooling anyplace she lived, but she read every book she could get, and learned fast. She was very smart for a virtually self-taught child.

When they crossed the border in 1919, Veneta, who was ten at the time, was left behind with her mother's friend Mrs. Titus, who had a new baby, Meredith, and needed someone to watch over the baby while she did the washing and cooking and all the other household duties. Mrs. Titus was very good to Veneta and wanted her her to stay as long as she could. She worked to make Veneta's visit a happy one, and was sad when time came for Veneta to rejoin her family.

The morning Veneta was leaving, Mrs. Titus pinned a paper on her to let everyone know she was going to the USA, and put her on a train to St. John. From there Veneta walked over the St. John Bridge and across the border to the American depot to catch the train to Cherryfield, Maine, near Millbridge, where she was to meet her mother.

The border men smiled and waved at the little girl carrying her suitcase with only a note pinned to her clothes, but they never stopped her from crossing into the country by herself. In fact there was a reporter there who took her photo on that trip and had it published in one of the local papers, a photograph that her mother had clipped and saved in a scrap book that had eventually gotten lost with so many other items.

Unfortunately, when Veneta reached the depot, the train she was to take to Cherryfield had already left. The baggage man, the only person there connected to the trains, told her the next one wouldn't be leaving until the following morning. He was visibly relieved when another young girl who had also been waiting took charge. She told Veneta not to be upset. "You can come home with me and I'll bring you back in the morning."

Veneta was nervous at the girl's house because it seemed such a dark place and she had a scary ill brother who behaved differently than other children. It was the only time she was actually frightened in all of her travels. But when she realized she was safe, she was grateful to be welcomed there, and to be fed and given a bed for the night. They woke her early in the morning and took her to the depot in time for the first train. When she arrived in Maine her mother was there calling and waving frantically. They were so glad to see each other.

It was a long distance by train from the Titus home to the bridge and then across the border to the station, especially for an unaccompanied ten year old. If you add the fact that she was crossing from her home country into another alien country with only a note pinned to her clothing and little else, the accomplishment must have seemed mountainous, enough for Veneta's memory of that moment to be a primary one. It was a coda, the ending of her life on the Robertson farm where she lived in the sunshine of the fields and watched her loved grandmother load her wagon for market and her grandfather tend the cows. She never returned to Canada after that, which means she never saw any of them again, not her grandparents or the blind dog Billy Jigs, or the cows and the farmhands, and never gathered up her precious bits of glass hidden safely under the corner of the barn. Missing her train and having to go home with strangers could only have made the journey more traumatic, suspending her in such an unfamiliar limbo overnight. Her relief and joy when she saw her mother waving frenetically at the station in Cherryfield must have seemed almost tactile to anyone looking on, as it must to the readers of this book, and is to her children recording the event.

While Veneta had been with the Titus family, Veneta's parents had settled at a logging camp where Martin worked logging and Annie May cooked for the men. That was where they lived when Veneta was reunited with them all. But logging was dangerous work, pushing all those logs where one could easily be crushed, especially during the logjams. It was not a place where one would raise young children. Once again Annie May had to find a house to rent. They settled in Millbridge, Maine, right next to a sardine cannery, the Eagle Preserve Fish Company. It was an interesting place where once a year all the residents could take an empty wheelbarrow to the cannery and fill it up with cans of sardines.

After they lived by the factory, they found a house for a few dollars a month on a dead-end street on the other side of town and past the cemetery. That may have been the house where Hazel, Veneta's very pretty and bright aunt, came and delivered a baby in the attic in 1922. They named the baby Mona and she became one more child Annie May agreed to raise as her own.

Before they moved into that house, they had been told they were not to touch any of the things that were stored in a second building on the property. In spite of that, at Christmastime Edgar didn't see any harm in taking a few toy containers from that building, since they didn't seem to be of such great value and there had been so many of them. He gave each of the younger children a small glass car or train filled with candy. Up until that time they were happy with an orange and an apple, and maybe a homemade gift in their stockings.

When the sheriff came to the house in the middle of the night looking for the responsible party, he went up into the attic where all the children were sleeping and looked under the blankets. "They are all kids," he told the others and they left, evidently looking for signs of Edgar and Martin outside. After no luck they returned to the house, took the kids downstairs, lined them up and arrested eleven year old Bill, the oldest boy there. They charged him with stealing the glass candy containers. Veneta remembered standing there with her mouth open, not believing they would actually take her brother away. He was such a good kid, rather small and thin for his age, and he didn't even complain at the time, or when he was subsequently held in prison for a year.

We will never know the complete truth about that incident. But we do know that arresting an innocent eleven-year-old was serious child abuse, even if the sheriff only took him believing that would force Martin or Edgar to give themselves up. Fortunately, Bill was a survivor. In spite of that experience, he grew up to be a solid citizen, years later even joining the Royal Air Force where he became a top marksman. And when he was in the States he spent a tour in the army.

Veneta's younger sister Bernice recalled that Annie May once carried food to Martin and Edgar in the woods following the candy container incident. After that, Edgar must have gone to Newark, New Jersey, where he heard there were ample work opportunities. The only time Martin was seen again was when he once visited Veneta at Aunt Agnes' in Haverhill. Veneta remembered his visit, and though she loved him, she wouldn't

Annie May 'horsing around' with friend at logging camp where she worked as a cook.

Edgar in the back, Veneta, Georgie and Bill in middle, and little Carl down front.

Veneta in New Jersey in the early 1930s.

Frank, Sidney Glasburg, the trainer, and Willy Pep.

talk to him. It would have been natural for her to feel that he had abandoned them all, particularly Bill. But Annie May, who also still loved him, always hoped that he would come home. And in spite of being told they had found a body on a river bank that matched his description, she never believed that was him and continued to add his name to the census for more than ten years.

These events were major to the family and Veneta's journey. First there was the loss of her father, a man they all loved, which precipitated all the other things that followed. Edgar, who had been such a dependable older brother, was also out of their lives for a while, even though Annie May managed to keep in touch with him. Bill, the closest to Veneta, was still in jail and out of touch. The rest of the children were again scattered to stay with family until Annie May managed to find a place for them all. It was tragic that such an insignificant theft of a few candy containers could cause such upheaval in a family.

Georgie went to stay with Aunt Lena and Uncle Mike, but Georgie was growing older and even more strong-willed. None of the family managed to keep her very long. Veneta, a more placid child, went to Haverhill. Her aunt and uncle lived on the top floor of a multi-family and both worked in the shoe factory that was the main industry in Haverhill at the time. Agnes and Walter were wonderful to her. And they clearly loved their children. Aunt Agnes would lift them up on her lap, hug them, and ask them all about their day.

Annie May showed up on two occasions to take Veneta on a holiday. Once they went to Bar Harbor and stayed in Mr. Robinson's barn for two weeks, right there on the coast. The barn backed right up to the water. They had a grand time. The second holiday was a steamship ride to a place Veneta later decided had been Nantasket Beach, an interesting coincidence since she presently lives not far from that steamship wharf.

Though she always enjoyed being with her Aunt Agnes, her memories of her days in Haverhill were not all good. She missed her family for one thing. And there was also the afternoon when she was in such a hurry after she washed the dishes and dried them off, she stacked them so high that she couldn't see where she was going and walked into a door jam on her way through to the dining room. The dishes crashed to the floor and broke into a thousand pieces.

Uncle Walter just laughed and said they needed a new set anyway, but Veneta was so upset she went to her room and didn't come out for a couple of days. Her Aunt Agnes had to bring her food and entice her into eating. Then when she did rejoin the family, her aunt was so glad to see her feeling better she took her into Boston and bought her an elegant dark red coat with fur around the collar and cuffs.

Aunt Agnes wanted Veneta to be happy and to stay with them forever. She took her to Harvard plays, and to Boston to shop for clothes when she needed them. She told her that she couldn't do without her, that she wouldn't trust anyone else with her little daughter Louise who Veneta tended.

By that time, when Veneta was a teenager, Annie May had joined Edgar where he was working in Newark, New Jersey, and together they arranged a place for all of them to live. Veneta remained in Haverhill while the others were settled in a neighborhood on Green Street, on the rough side of Newark. A man, with a cow or a pig, was murdered right near their house, but Edgar assured them that if they minded their own business they wouldn't be bothered. Newark was quite a place in those days.

Not too long after that, Annie May wrote to Veneta in Haverhill and asked if she would like to come home. She missed her daughter who never made a fuss and would help out. By then Veneta was sixteen, and it was the first opportunity since she had been a small child that she would have a chance to spend much time with her own family. That was also a big change. She was growing up.

When she arrived at Grand Central station, there was a young girl who was crying because she was feeling so lost and frightened, just as Veneta had been feeling as lost and frightened at the train station when she had missed the Cherryfield train years earlier. Coincidentally, the girl was also going to Newark, so Veneta, ignoring her own awe at being in such a immense place, comforted her and took the advice of a kindly conductor who suggested they take a cab. He also advised them to never talk to anyone who wasn't wearing a uniform. The two girls became close friends on the ride to Newark.

A short while after she arrived, she was taken by her siblings to Coney Island to go on the roller coaster for her seventeenth birthday. And soon after that she began work at Woolworth's big five-and-dime store. She was so well-read and well-spoken they saw she was smart in spite of her lack of education. It was a perfect place for her to work, not too far from her house and, more important, she loved the job and the independence that it allowed, even considering that most of her earnings had to help support the family. That was a happy time for her.

Georgie was attractive, with long beautiful blonde hair. She could make or fix anything. She could sew and cook, and taught the family to prepare and eat spaghetti. When she was around painting, cooking, sewing, or doing whatever needed doing, things would get accomplished. She was also a social butterfly, frequently going out to the clubs, even though she was underage. There was once a photo of her sitting on the hood of a car in the New York paper, right on the front page. The caption read *Beautiful Girl from Newark*. Another time, under another picture it said *Beauty from Newark*.

We heard that Bernice was the quietest of the girls, and that she was shy. And since she was younger than Georgie and Veneta, it was unlikely that she did any socializing with her friends in the Newark clubs.

Mona, the youngest of the Dupree girls, was a very sweet child. Everyone loved her. But she was not always well. A car had run over her foot while she was in Haverhill and it persisted in bothering her. She may also have had rheumatic fever, which was a serious illness that was treated with ice baths and rest. It was an illness that usually damaged the heart and might have been the factor that shortened her life.

Veneta remembered Edgar as being a great older brother, and very smart. But when he was in Newark he started to drink, usually on Friday nights. One night when he was very drunk and having difficulty finding his way home because the houses all looked the same, he mistakenly entered a neighbor's house. He was hungry and called for his mother to fix something for him. When she didn't respond he flipped the house apart. He pulled the sink off the wall, destroyed the stove and smashed all the furniture. He had done the same thing another time and was quite good at it.

Unfortunately, on that occasion, all the time he was wrecking everything a little boy was hiding under his bed in terror. Edgar fell asleep on top of that same bed with the poor boy trembling underneath. When the parents came home they heard Edgar moaning and groaning and calling for his mother. They believed Edgar was an honest man and understood that he had been too drunk to know what he was doing, and since their son was fine, and eventually everything repaired and put back, they forgave him.

Bill was still Veneta's best friend at that time. He had a motorcycle and sometimes he'd take her along on the back. One time he was shaken up when he had an accident riding by himself. Then later he had an accident at a very busy intersection on Main Street when Veneta was riding with him. They went down and slid through the intersection to the other side. Since there had been traffic moving in all directions, they were lucky they were not hurt seriously or killed. Understandably, Veneta wasn't too keen to ride after that, though she insisted she continued to love motorcycling.

Cookie remembered her mother frequently insisting she never wanted to see her daughters on the back of anyone's motorcycle, that it was too dangerous. That was curious, but possibly because there were so many bikes and so much traffic at the beach where they lived.

It was while Veneta was still at Woolworth's a few years later that Edgar's friend Frank, a handsome young prizefighter, saw her walking to work, and decided that she was just the girl for him. By that time he had already been places and done things most young men hadn't even dreamed of doing. He had joined the army at the age of fourteen, at Camp Murray, in Washington. From there he was sent to Nome, Alaska, where he was given a part in the first full-length movie shot entirely in Alaska, *The Chechahcos*. In the film he had to carry a barber's chair up the side of a mountain. That film also featured the greatest dogsled chase ever recorded. That all happened the same year Frank, even at his young age, became President Warren Harding's bodyguard during his tour of that territory. Unfortunately, the President became ill on his way from Alaska to California and died from ptomaine poisoning. Frank heard it was from eating bad crab meat.

When Frank had returned to his home in Washington

and been discharged, he had tried working several jobs before reenlisting, that time in the navy. He was sent by train to San Diego and then to the east coast. He set up fights with civilians all along the way. By the time he was out of the service, he had become the navy boxing camp. He was visible enough to impress the New Jersey boxing world and Sidney Glasburg, a new trainer. While he was with Glasburg he fought some big names, including sparring with Jack Dempsey, ending up New Jersey's *1927 Light Heavyweight Division Champ*—very impressive, since New Jersey was the center of the boxing world back then. He was good enough to eventually became known as the Knockout King of Saint Nick.

Shortly after Frank had noticed Veneta, he decided she was the one he was going to marry. He would stand across the street and watch her going to work every day, until Edgar, a great fight fan, brought him home to meet her. Veneta continued to work at Woolworth's, and was putting in extra hours doing inventory one day when the frantic store manager came and told her that Frank was outside with a brick he threatened to throw through the front window if the manager didn't send his girl out.

"Oh, Veneta, what am I going to do?"

In spite of loving her job, she knew what was what. "Oh, that's okay," she told the manager, "I'll just go home so that there won't be any trouble."

Frank and Veneta were married in 1927. A few years later, in the summer of 1931 when they were walking their first baby, Sidney, in his carriage, along came her old boss with his new wife and baby, but they just walked on by as if they didn't even know each other. For a long time she wondered why they had never even stopped to talk and compare their new infants.

Though they all loved the excitement, Veneta frequently wondered if it would have been better if she had never gone to Newark. Her mother always had it difficult; her brother Bill, her best companion, was always off on his motorcycle; and she met Frank and rushed too quickly into marriage. Of course, some of the notoriety from his successes in the ring rubbed off on her, and that was very special. For instance, there was one time when she was in Madison Square Garden for a cyclorama and she was asked to stand and be introduced to the crowd. "We have with us today, in the audience, Frank Willis's beautiful wife, Veneta." There was a rousing moment of applause and a standing ovation.

Veneta's younger sister, Bernice, remembers tagging along with Frank everywhere, even to political rallies where he was in great demand. She was just at that perfect age to tag along. She enjoyed the attention and the gatherings of people wherever they went.

Another time, Frank went back to his home in Washington to visit with his family. He sent for Veneta and she traveled across the country by train, and loved it from the moment she boarded in Grand Central Station until she stepped down in Tacoma, Washington. And once on the train, the railroad personnel and the other passengers had been friendly and helpful, especially one

This is possibly an update of the actual farm stand Veneta arrived at when she was following the crows to her cousin's farm.

Booth Bay Harbor where Annie May took Veneta on a holiday. Note the sign on the barn. Robertson's Boat Shop.'

young man who was so overwhelmed by her he wouldn't let her lift a piece of luggage. By the time they reached Washington, he was professing his adoration, which was very flattering.

To add to the pleasure of the train ride itself, when she reached Frank's family home, she quickly became attached to her in-laws, particularly her mother-in-law, Orange, who seemed like the perfect grandmother. Orange kept the books for her church and worked making smocks for the Japanese people, and on other charitable projects to which the church was connected.

When Frank was called back to Newark for training, Veneta chose to stay in Washington with his parents for a few extra months. She wouldn't have had a chance to see much of Frank in any case, since his trainer, Sidney, didn't think it was good for a fighter to have anything but training on his mind just before a fight, and he ran the show.

Frank thought Glasburg was the greatest trainer/manager, and felt lucky to have him. He also trained and managed Willie Pep, a featherweight who, in spite of his size, was considered to be one of the best fighters of the century. It was a sad day for Frank and all the fight fans when Sidney Glasburg was hit by a car and killed in Florida.

Annie May moved to Massachusetts with Bernice and Mona to stay with Mr. Benedict in Hingham. Mr. and Mrs. Benedict had been her old friends before Mrs. Benedict passed away in 1925. Mr. Benedict offered them living space in his home on railroad property where he was the track switchman at Nantasket Junction.

Georgie had married a nice man named Nick Schaub. But after a couple of years she threw her things in a suitcase, took the kids, one boy and one girl, and left him to join her mother. By then Annie May was doing very well working for the rich families there. But Georgie was never happy in Hingham and soon moved to Brockton, which was a bit more urban and exciting.

Veneta and Frank also moved up to Massachusetts with their little boy Sidney, and their little daughter Diane, born in New Jersey a year and a half after her brother. With his trainer gone, the move may also have been because Frank was retiring from the ring and needed to start new somewhere.

They settled with Annie May at the Benedicts' in Hingham. That was where their youngest daughter Cookie was born in 1933. She was delivered by Frank in the light from car headlights. A neighbor had pulled his car close to a house window to compensate for the loss of electricity during an intense electrical storm. The doctor had arrived only in time to cut the cord.

Since trains and young children were not a good combination, Veneta and Frank were concerned about the proximity of the tracks. As a result they moved up to the Bouve Mansion, also in Hingham. They lived in the servants' quarters on the estate while Veneta and Annie May helped Mrs. Bouve pack up the china and things. That was following the senior Mr. Bouve's death, when the family was preparing the house to be sold. The young Mrs. Bouve, who played piano in one of the churches at West

Corner, loved Annie May and was wonderful to Veneta while they worked for her. Her father-in-law had been an important military man. And his son owned a successful business on the harbor.

When they left the Bouves', Frank and Veneta moved to Cherry Street and Annie May moved to Canterbury Street. Edgar had one of his temper tantrums one Friday night, again because his mother was wasn't around to cook for him. During his rage, he rolled her oak kitchen table down the street, where it may still be. Maybe it rolled to the very end where the body was buried.

That was a startling thought even after Dale explained that it wasn't a secret body, just an odd place for an unmarked family burial plot. Dale wondered if they were still there—the table and the body.

Edgar left after that. He married a nice woman named Florence and adopted her son, Billy Gibbons. The one story that we heard about Billy was of the day Edgar was sitting reading his paper when he was startled by the noise of someone hammering. Young Billy was pounding nails through the carpet into the floor. Billy did unexpected things, though he was usually very easygoing. He was in many ways very like Edgar who was also easygoing most of the time. They were also both shorter and huskier in build, the boy like a miniature of the man. Unfortunately, also like him, he was occasionally gruffly destructive.

Veneta, Frank and their kids still lived on Cherry Street

when little Cookie fell into a small pool of water on the edge of a wooded area across the street. She had the good fortune to be pulled out by one of the older boys, Jackie Thompson, from up the road. That was one area that attracted the kids in the neighborhood. A second area was a candy store in a gas station across the lower edge of the property, just beyond the stone wall and the road to West Corner. The store had a clock over it that Frank had sold to the owner when he was working for IBM for a short time during the depression. And inside the gas station were cases of all kinds of candy, Tootsie Rolls and licorice sticks and lollypops and every other sort of sweet. And best of all, Sidney and Diane were given permission to cross the street if they looked both ways, and were especially careful.

Frank was an honest and good man. For one thing, his family always came first. He worked hard and managed to earn money even when jobs were scarce. He made and sold soap, potato chips and root beer during the depression. And when things were better he got a job at the local shipyard as a pipe bender. That was when they planned to buy the house and all the land attached. Unfortunately he dropped a heavy pipe on his foot at work and had to have a toe removed. Without work for the duration of his recovery, he could not buy the house and they ended up moving to upper Canterbury Street, nearby.

The house the family moved into was directly across the street from the little one room school that Sidney and Diane attended. It was on a drive that ended in a cul-de-sac where the kids could all play safely. There was another family, the Sargents, who lived across the drive, and behind them there was a fenced pasture where they kept their cows. The white-haired, bearded grandfather Sargent and his wife lived with one son in a house just beyond Veneta and Frank's house.

The Thompsons, Anna, Joe, Mary and Jack and their parents, lived at the upper end of the drive. Anna, the same age as Veneta's Diane, had a playhouse and a real live rabbit. The rabbit lived under the playhouse, where it was relatively safe from both predators and too energetic children. The rabbit and the children were all also safe from traffic, making it a great place for games and riding their tricycles and wagons. Sometimes Sidney played with them too, but more often he was with the other boys who gathered on that drive in closer proximity to the pasture.

Some of the older boys were not always well behaved. For one thing, in the evenings they would occasionally sneak into the grandfather Sargent's rhubarb patch and pull up lots of the rhubarb. They said it was because he had imbedded glass in the cement on the top of the stone walls to keep them out. And he said he imbedded the glass to keep them from pulling up his rhubarb. That was too sad.

Those boys also liked to panic the cows until they stampeded and jumped the fence, though Sidney and the younger ones only stood on the swinging pasture gate to watch the action. Unfortunately, one of the cows tried to jump the fence and didn't make it, and that sobered everyone up. The kids never harassed the cows again.

All the children in the neighborhood benefited from Frank's

craftsmanship, and most of the things he created were safer than some of the things sold in the stores, and more fun. One thing he taught them all to do was fold tin cans up around their sneakers, with rope run through them to hang onto while they clopped up and down the driveway like noisy horses. And one year he made stilts for everyone, the neighbor kids too, tall ones for the older kids and short ones for the little ones. They had a lot of fun learning to walk around on them. He also made a wagon for Sidney and baby cradles for Diane and Cookie, and skis and a guitar and many other things. For Veneta, he made a barbecue pit out of an old oil drum so they could have the neighbors over for cookouts, usually after the kids were off to bed.

Veneta had friends in that neighborhood, the Thompsons and the Sargents, and several others. Everyone liked her. She enjoyed taking craft classes with the other mothers, at the small school across the street. One year she painted a metal doorstop that they had forever. She was always making things, sewing curtains and bedspreads, and clothes for the children. She loved keeping them and the house clean and pretty.

There were lots of stories about that time. When Sidney had gone on to a larger school, and Diane had settled in across the street, Cookie, refusing to be left out on her own, went over and kicked on the school door until they let her in, and stayed, the youngest student they had ever had in that small school room. In spite of the nurse's protest, with the teachers consent they tested her and decided she could skip kindergarten and officially start first grade in the fall, just one year instead of two behind Diane, who had been the youngest up until then. That left Veneta with her mornings free for the first time, which, from the look of the house, she spent scrubbing and polishing and sewing and baking. And possibly she even walked up the drive to visit with her friend Mary Thompson.

There were firefly hunts on hot summer evenings. Fourth of July was celebrated with new cap pistols for the kids and sparklers to be swirled in the air, and food cooked on the oil can barbeque. And the neighbors would join them to eat and talk. If they were lucky they would all go to see the fireworks and the bonfire at one of the schools.

Sidney also remembered when the iceman had a fit on his way down to West Corner with a full load of ice in his horse-drawn wagon and threw all the ice in the street. He was swearing a streak all the way back up Rockland Street to his icehouse in back of his home. All the kids in the neighborhood were thrilled. They clamored for the hunks of ice to suck on for the rest of that hot afternoon.

In the winter they skated on a little frozen pond at the upper end of Canterbury Street. Veneta would watch from the side while Frank tried to teach the little ones to skate on the double runners, and later on the single blades. None of them did very well, but their cheeks would be crimson and they were all happy.

Sidney also remembered winters when they would close one side of the road so the kids could slide down the hill safely. And one time Frank made a bobsled that sat about six of the neighborhood fathers. They poured water down the hill until it was all ice and then rode the bobsled down at breakneck speed, miraculously making it to the bottom without anyone getting killed. Maybe even a couple of the mothers got brave enough to try out the bobsled as well. We believe the police department came and stopped that action by reopening the road and sanding and giving them all a warning not to ever do it again.

While they lived in that house, Sidney, Diane and Cookie, as well as Anna and Joe Thompson became the Black Mask Gang. Sidney was the leader and Cookie, the youngest, the tagalong. The Black Mask Gang was always off on one adventure or another. During one of those occasions Sidney climbed the abandoned tower at the old abby located on the Hingham side of Hull Street. He collected broken bits of stained glass he found there, glass in all colors that they believed were jewels. They were, after all, very young. So they put the jewels in a container and buried it like a treasure in a hole they dug under a tree in the front yard of the house across from their own.

Diane says that whenever she drives up that way she feels like sneaking into that yard and digging that treasure up, or at least seeing if it still exists.

The Black Mask Gang members were lucky they survived some of their adventures. There was, for instance, a cave that went under some rocks in the woods. They would crawl into that cave and it eventually became their meeting place. They were lucky they didn't get stuck, or have the rocks tumble in on them, or run into some animal who had chosen that as a den.

Veneta always had a ready hand for anyone in difficulty.

Edgar, Frank and Bill in New Jersey.

Veneta's younger brother Bill in the Army in the States.

Veneta and Frank in Newark.

Frank, Edgar and a friend Jim spar while young fans copy their moves.

That was one thing she and Frank had in common. One year, for instance, she had gotten to know a family who had lost their home because the father was sick and could not work. Veneta pressured Frank, and Frank gathered the neighbors together to renovate an old condemned house, 73 Canterbury Street. Everyone worked together stripping paper, re-papering, painting, repairing the place inside and out until it was beautiful. In fact, when they painted the outside a sunny yellow with white trim, it was the prettiest house on the street. It also had a great porch that extended all across the front. There was a barn out back and lots of usable land around it, and a neat stone wall along the front of the yard with honeysuckle, tiger lilies and daisies growing wildly along the base.

The family moved in gratefully and lived there for two or three years before they moved into a house they bought in a different neighborhood. Veneta, Frank and the children moved in before anyone else had a chance to even consider it.

That was the house Veneta most loved. There were plenty of rooms inside and even a fireplace in the parlor. Bernice came to live with them there. She was a young adult and just starting to date. Every time her friend showed up, she would hurry to hide her glasses up on the fireplace mantle in fear that her friend wouldn't see her beauty behind her spectacles.

In the summers Aunt Agnes would send her young daughter, Joyce, down from Haverhill to spend a few weeks. There were a couple of times that had not worked out well. Once the children told Joyce that you would never break out with poison ivy if you ate some. And to convince her, they all ate a few leaves. Joyce, who was highly allergic, happily went along with them, cautiously nibbling a leaf. Within days she was covered inside and out and the doctor had to make several house calls. Poor Joyce was the only one of them who had any reaction at all, and hers was almost critical.

Veneta always saw that her daughters got the very nicest dolls on Christmas and for their birthdays. Possibly she remembered how few gifts she had ever gotten as a child, and how desperately she had tried to rescue her only doll from the house that had burned to the ground. It had to have been as difficult for her as it was for her daughters when Joyce talked young Diane into giving her all their dolls. Diane never dreamed she would take them all back to Haverhill with her, and Veneta never insisted that she return them to the girls. I am sure that Joyce had no idea how much the dolls meant to Diane, and possibly she had few or none of her own. They were all too young to understand. Nonetheless, that was about as sad for Diane as it had been for Veneta when, in her childhood, the dog she treasured had been given away.

There were also times Veneta sent Diane or Cookie or Sidney up to spend some time with Aunt Agnes so they would get to know her and love her, just as she had when she was a girl. But Diane suffered from serious homesickness and always came back early. Cookie did a little better, but she was never really happy away from home, no matter how hard Aunt Agnes tried. She remembered how lonely it was trying to sleep out on the porch with Joyce because she could hear the train whistles in the middle of the night and they reminded her of how far away from home she was.

At the yellow house in Hingham, the barn with its hayloft was a great addition to their living. When their parents weren't renting the lower space to people who wanted a place to keep their cows, the kids were often in the loft jumping around or hiding in the hay. They also had room for the chickens Frank and Veneta raised so they could have fresh eggs, and hens for stewing. In the spring there was a good supply of baby chicks bursting out of their shells in the incubator. Veneta would let the kids each take an egg to hatch in a smaller incubator in one of the bedrooms, so they could keep watch on the whole process.

The first spring in that house, Veneta and Frank taught the kids to plant and grow vegetables. They let them each pick a packet of seeds and a part of the garden to plant in. Sidney and Diane, much smarter about such things, picked vegetables, carrots and peas and such, and dug and raked and seeded and weeded in a corner of their father's big garden. They were pleased when the seeds broke through the soil, and they were very attentive to the growing process. And though her parents tried to get her to reconsider, little Cookie chose to plant cucumber seeds in a crack in a large rock in the backyard. She must have gotten the idea from watching her mother and sister plant a rock garden in another part of the yard. So in the manner of planting a rock garden, she filled the crack with dirt and dropped in the *whole* packet of seeds, and watered while her parents looked on amused. Everyone's gardening was a great success. The vegetables were delicious at dinner, and to everyone's surprise Cookie's fat cucumbers grew wildly until they covered the whole rock.

Veneta and Frank canned all their own vegetables from the garden each year. They had jars of green beans and wax beans and relish and beets. And they pickled lots of cucumbers. Frank would can tomatoes and make his special catsup. And Veneta always made jars of grape jelly, and sometimes crabapple jelly. The kids helped by pouring the melted wax on the hot jelly to seal the top. Cooking the grapes always made the whole house smell good. That and all the lilacs and cutting flowers that were growing around outside, and filling vases inside.

Sidney got his first two-wheel bike when they lived in that house, and almost lost it again when he was caught giving a friend a ride on the bar. Riding double was frowned on and the local police would confiscate the bike of any kid caught doing that. Sid was lucky that he didn't lose his, but he did have to face his father's anger when he got home, and lose the right to ride for a week or so. And a couple of times, before he got home from school, one of his younger sisters added insult to injury by sneaking out his new bike and trying to ride it with some success. Trying to stop was harder and the bike ended up with a scraped up front fender, and his sister ended up with a couple of well-deserved bruises, from falling off the bike rather than from her brother's anger, which she might have deserved.

Cookie remembers how close she and Diane were as sisters learning to play Jacks and dressing and undressing dozens of paper dolls on that wonderful long porch. And all of them played in the woods behind the house as the Black Mask Gang, and hunted for foxes' dens, and walked to the library once a week, and down to West Corner every Sunday for church while Veneta stayed home and read in the quiet, and prepared dinner. The church was special to Frank, who made a beautiful three-foot high brass cross for the front altar. He made it using tools at the Fore River Shipyard where he worked. At the same time, he also made for the minister himself, an intricately designed small cross using burned matchsticks.

Wayne was born while they lived there. He was born in the Cohasset Hospital on Ripley Road, a special treat in those days of home deliveries. The rest of the kids would remember the day because, when they went to the hospital to see their new baby brother, the cat ate Diane's white mouse. That caused a row when they returned home, because she was sure the cat ate the mouse because her siblings made it happen. It seemed they were not too fond of her mouse. It was hard for Diane to forgive Sidney and Cookie, even though her father explained that the big yellow tomcat was capable of plucking it out of the cage all by himself.

It was only a short time after Wayne's birth that the owners of the yellow house decided to put it on the market. Because Frank and Veneta had brought the house back from being condemned, they had agreed to give Frank the option to buy, putting all their rent receipts together for a down payment. Unfortunately, Frank felt they were asking too much for a house that had once been condemned and that no one was interested in. He wanted to wait for a better deal. Sadly, with the start of the war the shipyard needed workers in a hurry, and to Frank's surprise, someone from Maine bought the house out from under them.

That was how they lost the house that the whole family loved. Veneta, who had been shuffled from place to place since she was a young child, needed to finally feel grounded in a place of her very own, and that house was nicer than any she had ever dreamt of owning.

Frank realized that he had made a serious mistake. In order to rectify that, he searched for another house and found one on Park Avenue in Hull, a small beach town a short distance away. Unfortunately, he didn't tell Veneta until he had actually purchased the place and presented it to her as an accomplished fact. Though it was a nice place, it didn't have all of the attributes of the yellow house. It had no barn in the back, no land for a large garden, and no close friends nearby. She was unable to hide her disappointment no matter what he did to make amends. And he did a lot. He plowed up the land to one side of the house after getting the people who owned part of it to agree to his adding that portion of their land to his garden. And he made renovations to the kitchen, built cabinets that helped modernize the space a bit.

For a while nothing made Veneta miss the yellow house less.

Standing in back--Frank & Annie May.
In front--Sidney, Diane, Cookie and
Billy Gibbons.

Bernice and Mona with Mr. Benedict
who was the track switcher at
Nantasket Junction.

Sid, Cookie and Diane with
neighborhood kids in the snow in
Hingham.

The Canterbury St. gang.
Back row: Frank, Bernice, Kenny, Mona,
Annie May.
Front row: Sidney, Billy, Cookie, Diane.

But it was the location of the new place that was most interesting. It was practically butting up against the back gate of Paragon Amusement Park, and only a block from the beach. It had, in fact, been one of the two Paragon Park houses: 28 Park Avenue belonging to the Stone family, who owned the park, and 30 Park Avenue belonging to the Cohen brothers, who owned the concession stands. That guaranteed plenty of visitors stopping to sit on the porch for a cup of tea after they walked sandy-footed up from the beach, or weary from a day at the park. Both family and friends spent their summers on that porch enjoying the crowds trudging past and the constant excitement of the beach itself.

For Veneta, being there was much like the fast-paced years in Newark, something she had missed. And being able to walk down the street to be submersed in the music and social interaction was a special sort of pleasure.

Her mother, Annie May, would come down and sit on the front porch, willing to read anyone's cards or just share a cup of tea. Bernice would show up on the back of her new husband's motorcycle and they would wander down along the beach before settling in for a visit.

Mona would often bring her guitar to play and sing while the kids and adults listened or joined in for a rousing western singalong. In spite of a continuing problem with her injured foot, she was a talented entertainer. She could yodel and sing Country Westerns in a sweet clear voice. She had married a young man named Kenny and sang with his band until they separated, and though she later remarried, she never regained her vitality or health.

Often, in the early morning, Veneta would walk down along the water's edge with a bucket and a small clamming rake and dig up quahog clams, which she would use for making the best New England clam chowder ever. Since she didn't swim and only moderately sunbathed, that was about the only time she ventured down along the beach that any of her children recalled. She preferred to dig in her garden and sit visiting on her front porch, or just stroll down along the avenue in the evening with friends.

Gardens were called Victory Gardens back then, because of the war. And their little garden was the best. Frank raised all the vegetables they needed during the growing months, including potatoes and celery and beets and all. The potato plants provided an endless supply of bugs that little Wayne would collect in old milk bottles. He would dump them out and count them every day, then put them back into the bottles for the night. It was an interesting little hobby for a toddler.

He was also a very bright tiny kid in lots of ways. He walked at six months and talked at a year, and looked even smaller when he would trot along hand in hand with his six-foot-three-inch dad most mornings. Frank would take him along when he went down to the cafe across from the police station for his morning coffee.

Sidney once told Dale that their father ran a card game in the foundation of one of the burned-out hotels on the ledges. Dale remembers the place was like an old fort. There were interesting things there, like the remains of an old shooting gallery with the ducks and things lying around on the floor. Apparently Frank was good with cards and saw that as a way of making more money for the family, until the games were closed down.

Once Frank tried to teach Veneta how to drive, but that was a disaster. He had little patience because he was always afraid he'd be late for work, or some other pressing thing. "Go ahead, drive it!" he'd say, without explaining how she was to go about it. After several attempts, she decided she didn't want to have anything to do with cars. He could have them for himself. It almost seemed to her that he didn't want her to learn. And that may have been a fact.

When Wayne was about three, Frank felt compelled to go off to war with the other men who were enlisting from his state guard unit. That led him to a foxhole in Europe during the Battle of the Bulge, and a lot of acts of bravery. At one time, for instance, when he was caught behind enemy lines, he carried a badly wounded soldier who had been machine gunned in both legs, twenty miles to safety. He turned him over to another man, who was sadly and wrongly given credit for that courageous action. That man tried to correct the mistake, and he wrote Frank a letter letting him know that. Frank also received a letter from the man he had saved, and his family. (While he was in that foxhole, during the calm moments, he hand crocheted some tiny booties for his third son, Dale, who was born during his absence.)

Wayne spent much of his three-year-old time standing on an orange crate in the middle of the driveway, directing an imaginary orchestra. Veneta would see that one of the girls, Diane or Cookie, would wheel him and his orange crate in his stroller down onto the boardwalk of the Nantasket Hotel, where a band concert was held every Saturday, Sunday, and Wednesday. Sometimes the band conductor would even wait while Wayne stepped up on the crate on the balcony overlooking the band, so they could begin directing together. That made Wayne happy and always pleased the crowd.

Veneta was on her own with four children and not a lot of money coming in. The government sent a monthly check that only meagerly covered three dependents, when there were five, including Veneta. The first thing she did was get the upstairs rooms ready to rent out in the summertime. That meant painting every room in the house with a water-based paint that had a very distinctive almost pleasant odor. The older kids all pitched in. And Veneta herself, dressed in slacks and a man's old white shirt, and sneakers or her platform shoes, did more work than anyone else.

The second thing she did was get a job in the kitchen of Miss Crowley's rooming house, one road over. She also took in ironing and scrubbed floors. And the girls helped by earning their own spending money by babysitting and working handing out towels at the bathhouses. And the boys worked at the park and doing odd jobs. It all helped.

As Sid grew older he worked several places, including at Leo's, a small restaurant across from the beach, and setting pins in the bowling alley. But his favorite thing was clam digging, though he almost got caught in the quicksand one time when he was clamming near Riggor's Rock. Then there was the time he was working on one of the steamships that came in and out of the harbor bringing the tourists down from Boston, and learned that all the cooks on the ships were Duprees. When they heard his mother had been one as well, they fed him and treated him like a king. They told him that a number of times they had taken Annie May on one of their trips, once with Veneta along. That explains why Veneta felt she had been in that town when she went on a holiday with her mother.

They had a little black and white short-haired dog at that time, a terrier mix. His name was Speedy, which was a great name for a little dog that didn't speed very far or very often. He may have originally been Sidney's dog, but mostly he stuck close to Veneta or any one of the kids who were at home to inadvertently give him a pat, or shift over on the couch so he could sneak up for a close moment. He was a good, quiet little creature who just seemed to be content to be there.

Since the beach was a wonderful vacation spot, the rooms rented easily and no one seemed to mind that the furnishings were well used. Everything was spotlessly clean, the bedding freshly laundered and the rooms airy. All of the neighbors began to rent their rooms as well and were very supportive of each other, loaning sheets and towels during particularly busy weeks as well as sending each other roomers when their own places were filled.

It was an exciting time, when the war was still on and all the young servicemen crowded the beach on their last leaves before shipping out. Most of them were sailors in their summer whites, young kids who had planned to sleep on the beach, until they found out the beaches were out of bounds at night in those days. They were patrolled by the coastguard to make sure no enemy saboteur paddled to shore from some u-boat submerged out in the shipping lanes. That left the stranded young servicemen sleeping on lawns and porches up and down the side streets, and even on the floor of Veneta's front room, so they wouldn't get picked up. There was a constant turnover of families from Boston as well, and from out of state, people who left happy and put in their reservations for the following summer before they packed up their cars.

And there were regulars who spent the whole summer, like the three waitresses who came to make the big tips working in the restaurants or nightclubs down on the avenue. It was fun for them, because they spent time on the beach in the daytime and worked and partied all night. And they became friends with Veneta, who needed company she could laugh and occasionally go places with. One of them, Dolly, became Veneta's best friend

Georgie's children, Babs, Joyce, Ronald and Kenny, who were at Veneta's house during the scarlet fever epidemic.

Frank, in France on his way to Germany during the Battle of the Bulge. He was proud to have served in the 100th division there.

Mona, as she looked when she was playing guitar and singing for everyone on Veneta's front porch at the beach.

Veneta and Georgie painting the windows on the Park Avenue house.

and was like family. She kept in touch even after she married and could only come to the beach for short visits in the summers.

Winters at the beach were long and cold, some winters longer than others. For instance, there was the year when Wayne was still the youngest, that stressful time when Sidney came down with scarlet fever in December and was sent to the hospital for infectious diseases in Boston. That was a scary time, made more so because Veneta was reminded of her three brothers who were lost to serious illnesses as babies. Life was hazardous at best.

That was also the winter when Georgie, who had returned to New Jersey to settle down and raise her family, came north to stay at Veneta's small house at the beach with her four children. Her youngest son Kenny was dreadfully ill with asthma and needed treatment at the Children's Hospital in Boston. Unfortunately, as Kenny was ambulanced to one hospital in Boston, Sidney was ambulanced home from another hospital, more ill than he had been when he went there. He was malnourished and sick with pneumonia, the dregs of his ailment, and still as contagious as ever. A large yellow SCARLET FEVER quarantine sign was posted on the porch to forbid anyone to enter or leave that bastion of infection.

And since there were eight children, including Kenny, who was back and forth from the hospital a couple of times, and one adult ill in a connected line from the beginning of winter until the spring, the number considered sufficient to pronounce the outbreak in that one house an epidemic, the town was forced to close the schools for a period of time. That made all the kids in town happy, but it also left the Willis and Schaub children isolated and incarcerated for an insufferably long time.

There was scant food, though the local grocer did deliver basic supplies somewhat often. And there was bread regularly left on the front porch by the bakery, but it was old bread already smelling of mold. There were beds to change and heads to ice down. And someone given special dispensation since they were not yet noticeably ill, had to walk all the way down the avenue, no matter how wintery the weather, to pick up medicine, while making minimum contact through the drugstore door. The pharmacist was a kind man who often sent treats for the kids.

When Georgie became ill too, that left Veneta to handle all the nursing and nourishing chores. It was fortunate that she had a mild case of the fever when she was a child, and had built up a protective immunity to the disease. The town did very little to help make things easier, no nurse or nursing assistance during the worst of things. Everything was dependent on Veneta. And to add to that, unknown to her children at the time, she was pregnant with her third son.

Dale was the most beautiful baby with the brightest eyes and sweetest smile. He always smelled as clean and sweet as all of Veneta's children did. And the greatest pleasure the girls experienced was lying beside him on the bed and just watching him sleep or kick his little booties off. (Interestingly, Dale still has the booties Frank hand crocheted for him while keeping warm in that foxhole during the Battle of the Bulge.) He was also a bright, headstrong baby who grew up to be a bright, even more headstrong child.

When Gary was born some years later, he was a perfectly sweet little baby, all smiles and gentleness and not concerned more than normal about his world. He grew rapidly and, before anyone knew it, he was assimilated into the Willis beach gang, taking his rightful place as the youngest in the family. Wayne and Dale seemed happy to add a new little brother to their ranks. The three of them loved to go to the dump and find anything with wheels on it. Dale said that Mom dreaded to see them coming over the hill, knowing they would probably be pushing an old broken down carriage that they intended to make into a car, or once a bus, with all the parts they had gathered. He remembers how they rode the homemade bus with three other kids, six in all, down Berkley Road and crashed in the turn towards Atherton when they hit sand. He felt the design was perfect, but they didn't know that they had to put out their feet to slow down for the corner.

One of the great experiences for the boys was meeting the families that put on the animal shows in the center of the amusement park. They had all sorts of animals, seals, dogs, ponies, and even trained elephants. And even more wonderful, the performers occasionally let the boys lead the ponies out to the performance area. Dale still remembers the show music that accompanied them. It was a perfect experience for three young kids.

For years Veneta and Dolly, the young waitress who had rented a room every summer for a number of years, had remained in touch. When Dolly was married and involved with raising a family, they made do with shorter visits and longer phone calls. They shared the news about their families and mutual friends and their pleasant experiences, and their less pleasant ones. For instance, Veneta talked about her divorce, their having been separated so long by the war, and how Frank had remarried in Japan and had another child, Linda; how she felt okay about all of that.

They talked about Diane and Cookie's marriages, both too young, and how Diane ended up very ill with hepatitis when her first child, a little boy, was born. Dolly in turn told about her husband's illness and her daughter's marriage, and other things.

They shared concerns when Sidney went into the service, and the horribleness of all that. He was a lineman in Korea, and the stress, seeing so many of his army buddies killed by snipers who liked to pick them off the poles as if it were a macabre game, took its toll. Veneta told Dolly how he had met up with Frank there, and they had gotten to know each other again during their times spent in Japan.

She told Dolly the less important things, how she had dreamed about Cookie cutting her hair, and was so distressed the next day to find out she actually had done that. And she shared the more important things, like her pain when little Gary caught polio during the epidemic when he was only five and how he spent six

Sidney, Veneta's oldest son, saw action in Korea, and spent time with Frank in Japan where his father was stationed.

Veneta, as an auntie and a grandmother. and a great-grandmother

Veneta, Sid, Barbara, Diane, Wayne. and Todd in Bennington, New Hampshire.

Five generations!
Baby Kayleigh, Diane (great grandmother, nicole (Mother), Jean ((grandmother), and Veneta (great-great grandmother.)

months in a hospital in Boston. And how he came home partially paralyzed along one side and refused to use his crutches when he went out to chase after his brothers.

She admitted to Dolly that as much as she loved babies, she, who only reluctantly admitted she had grown children, hated to be called a *grandmother*. She even hesitantly accepted being called an *auntie* when there was no other choice.

All that time she had her three youngest sons living at home and catered to them in the same manner her mother had catered to her brothers. And as they grew she had little reason to regret that. Wayne went into the navy and eventually came home weary and much wiser. Dale also eventually did a tour of duty, in the the navy as well. He came home and married a high school sweetheart. Gary, the youngest, also a navy man, had neglected to tell the recruiters about the polio. He married after his return home as well. Wayne stayed single for a number of years before he married.

From those unions came the grandchildren. Sidney, who became a famous artist, and his artist wife, Barbara, had two boys. Diane, a talented seamstress/artist, and her lobster fisherman husband had five children, a boy and four girls. Cookie, an author and painter, married an ex-marine/student and they also had five children, four girls and boy. Wayne, a carpenter and skilled carnival technician, kept the park running smoothly for lots of years and eventually married and had one son. Dale, who started a painting company, and his wife Donna had two boys. And Gary, a railroad engineer, and his artist wife had two boys.

And most of those grandchildren eventually had children of their own, and those great grandchildren had children, Veneta's great great grandchildren, and so on.

During those years Veneta had taken a job at a bag factory in a nearby town. It was hard work, but she enjoyed the people she worked with. Unfortunately, the chemicals in the glues took a toll. Much later, in her eighties, she was losing her sight. It was interesting that she knew that was going to happen, and a couple of years before it did she began to memorize her house, walking through it and doing her chores with her eyes closed until she had all of it solidly in her head. But when she could no longer see the physical beauty of life, the sunsets, and flocks of birds flying in long lines toward Canada, the beautiful turning of the leaves in fall, the darkness began to subdue the laughter that was such a special greeting when you entered her kitchen, or walked up her front steps.

Fortunately, Dale was able to gradually take over her care. And under his gentle watch she began to regain some of her health. She is over a hundred now as this is being written. There are many moments when we see her smile, and hear her soft-spoken words. And when you take her hand and she connects with you, there is that joy of recognition. And if she gives you enough of her presence, sometimes a shared memory reconnects the laughter and being there is good.

We hope that this little book will remind anyone reading it of Veneta when she would smile shyly with strangers, and

Veneta who would sit on her front porch and welcome anyone up for a chat, who loved her friends even when they were gone for years. And help them remember how she loved to dance, especially with her granddaughter Jean's son Mark, at all the family weddings, how she would giggle after two sips of wine or beer or champaign. And remember how her face would light up when Dickie or Sean or Lisa, or any of the others, family and friends, came to call, and how she opened her house to anyone needing a place in the sun.

VENETA'S DESCENDANTS

Justin William Waitkus

Sarth Larkin

Monique (Reilly) Cole

Diane (Willis) Figueiredo

Adam Fredrick Kapp

Gary Paul Willis

Frank Larkworthy

Jeremy David Fullerton

Hunter William Figueiredo

Tristan Mckenzie Beale

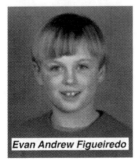

Evan Andrew Figueiredo

Madisyn Taylor Rossi

Risa Sandra Kapp

Nicholas Jordan Fullerton

Heidi Jean McLore

Nicole Savitski

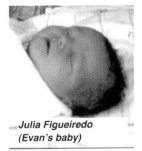

Julia Figueiredo
(Evan's baby)

Cameron Alexis Fullerton

Mark McLore

Meta (Kapp) Thorndyke

Jerry Dale Willis

Gracie Figueiredo

Ethan William Fife

Adria Leigh Figueiredo

Diane L. Fullerton

Kayleigh Savitski

Patty Larkin

Richard Figueiredo

Geri Larkin

Jared Dana Waitus

Kathy McLore Yudis

Ryan Reilly and Baby Cody

Zachary Cormier

Dylan Cormier

Nicole and Heidi

Lee Frances Baker

David Neal Willis

Dale Anthony Willis

Sidney Frank Willis

Tara Beale

Jonathon James Fife

Dick Figueiredo & Cory

Jamie Larkin-Markus

Deiter Willis

Linda (Willis) Ford
and baby Colin

Kym Waitkus

Steven Mark McLore

Ben & Greta Vee Willis

Matthew Dana Fletcher

Elizabeth Willis

Shane Cormier

Taite Beale

Brett Sak

Beau Larkin

Todd Willis

Sharleen (Willis) Kapp
'Cookie'

Jonathon Reid Fife

Chrissy McLore Gonsalves

Matt Fletcher in uniform

Sean Willis

Michael William Sak

Ashley Savitski

Sandy Fletcher

Brandin Nicholas Waitkus

Wayne L. Willis

Ryan Paul

Jean McLore

Steve Kapp

Colin Douglas Fletcher

Three members of the Black Mask Gang

Wayne and his son David
on the merry-go-round in
Paragon Park.

Annie May Robertson,
Veneta's mother

Veneta's sister Bernice

Veneta, Mary , Monique, Lee, Bob, Diane Billy

Sidney, Cookie & Diane on
a stonewall in Hingham.

John with black eyes

Veneta, on Billy's lobster
boat, enjoying the warm
early spring.

Ryan & Jon

THE FROZEN GOOSE
A Memory from Veneta's Childhood

Once upon a time, as all stories are supposed to begin, about ninety-six years ago when Veneta was six years old, she lived on a farm in Canada, in a place where the winters were so cold that the world outside looked like her storybook picture of the North Pole. They didn't have many animals on the farm, mostly cows and chickens, a couple of goats, one large sheep and one very large pig. And several noisy geese. The chickens and the geese lived in a coop which was like a little building attached to the side of the barn with a little door so they could run in and out when they needed water and food. The other animals lived in the barn itself, except for the pig that had a place all to himself, a lean-to attached to the back of the barn.

During the good weather it was Veneta's job to feed chickens and the geese and the pig. She would toss scraps to the pig and put scoops of mash in the food trough, and water in the water trough. The chickens and geese also had food and water troughs in their sections of the farmyard.

Veneta loved feeding the animals—all except one goose who would run at her with its wings high on each side and its neck stretched out full, honking in that angry honking sound that makes geese such good watchdogs on farms like her family's. That goose could drive away the worst animal or hungry hobo trying to raid the coop.

And it could drive away the littlest girl trying to scatter feed or retrieve eggs or fill water troughs. That's why she always fed the chickens and geese last and sometimes not at all, even though her mama said the mean old goose wouldn't hurt her if she just flapped her apron at her and told her to shoo. "She's just trying to show you who's boss." But her apron wasn't as big and floppy as her mama's, so the goose remained the boss and most days mama had to finish feeding them for Veneta while she shivered by the stove, trying to warm herself and calm herself at the same time. It was a fact that the goose didn't like Veneta and Veneta didn't like that goose.

One very cold morning, much colder than all the other mornings had been, when Veneta had eaten the last bit of her hot oatmeal sweetened with dribbles of sweet molasses, she bundled up in her warmest outdoor clothes, wrapped her long wool scarf around her neck, and pulled her tam o' shanter hat, the one her grandma had knitted for her, so far down on her head it covered her ears. She buckled up her black galoshes, put on her mittens that swung at the ends of the string that passed up one arm of her jacket down the other, and tugged open the heavy front door.

The world was covered with white frost. Everything looked as though it were dusted with powdery sugar just like the gingerbread cakes mama made for holidays. And her breath blew out in puffy clouds in front of her face as she carried the scraps to the big old pig. He grunted a greeting at her but didn't move outside the lean-to the way he did most mornings. Veneta noticed that his water was frozen into a solid lump. When she gave mash to the sheep and the goats she saw that their water was also frozen. When her Pa and brothers were home they carried the heavy water buckets and took care of the ice, but when they were away at work and school her mother took care of all the frozen things.

Veneta had avoided the chicken coop with the open door, though she wondered why it was so quiet when she trudged along scattering grain and scraps across the chicken yard and into their food trough. The chickens hopped down their little ramp one at a time, scratching at the grain on the ground and tapping on the frozen water as if that would melt it down. Even the geese were slow about poking their heads out into the open. Veneta was very confused. Where was the mean old goose? Then she noticed a white lump lying by the water trough. The goose was flat on her back, her feet stuck out in one direction and her long neck in the other.

"Mama, Mama!" She ran into the house as fast as she could. "Mama, Mama! The goose…"

"Oh Veneta," her mother answered, believing that Veneta was going to tell her the goose had chased her again. "Take your things off and go warm up by the stove. I'll take care of the chickens and that nasty goose."

So while her mother bundled up and headed out the door, Veneta sat on the three-legged stool by the stove and unbuckled her boots. She could hear the wood snapping inside the firebox. Her mother had left the oven door ajar so more of the heat would spread out in the room. It seemed she hardly got the boot buckles all undone before she heard her mother bumping at the door.

"Veneta, hurry! Open the door and help me!"

"Mama, what has happened?" she asked, pushing the door wide so her mother could squeeze through.

"Get me a towel, dear. I found the big goose frozen stiff."

In her mother's arms, the goose was still stretched out like a board. "We'll wrap a towel around her and put her in the warm oven. Then we will wait and see what happens. But we must be very careful because the goose is so frozen she could break into pieces."

Veneta ran for a large towel and helped her mother wrap the goose carefully and place her, feet first, in the oven, her head partly poking out.

"Keep an eye on her, dear, while I see if any of the other animals are frozen," her mother said hurrying back out the door. "It will only take me a minute."

Veneta sat back down on the stool and finished unbuckling her boots. She couldn't stop staring at the goose. And as stiff as the goose was Veneta felt it was staring back. She wished her mama would hurry and not leave her alone with that mean old goose even if it was frozen stiff as a board. She carried her boots over to the box by the door and when she turned to look at the goose again there was water dripping out of its mouth.

"Mama! Mama! Hurry! There's water coming out of the goose's mouth." Veneta called out to her mother. "And dripping from her feathers!"

"That's wonderful," her mother called back as she hurried across the yard. "It means the goose is getting better."

"And look, Mama! The goose is moving," she pointed as her mama came in, shutting the door behind her.

"She sure is. Let's see if she can stand up and walk." Mama carefully lifted the goose out of the oven and set her down on the floor, loosening the towel.

"Look, Mama! The goose is walking! And the goose is flapping her wings and honking!" And indeed the goose was.

"Yes, Veneta, isn't it wonderful?"

"Yes, it is, Mama. It is wonderful!"

"This goose is a very lucky goose, Veneta. Let's put your coat back on and take this very lucky goose back outside with the other animals."

So Veneta put on her galoshes and her warm scarf and mittens, and pulled her tam o' shanter back down over her ears. She held the door open very wide while her mama shooed the lucky goose out into the yard.

"Will Lucky be fine now, Mama?"

"She should be. It's already getting warmer outside and tonight Papa will put more hay in the coop. And while we are outside we must break through the ice on the animals' water."

"I'll get a stick, Mama. Look, the other geese are coming to see Lucky."

"They are happy to see her. I'm sure they thought she was gone forever."

While Veneta was breaking through the ice with her stick the chickens and geese all gathered around waiting for a drink. And Lucky was there along with the rest, moving close to Veneta and never raising her wings or sticking out her neck or honking loudly. After that Lucky and Veneta became the best of friends, making that experience and that cold winter a special one to remember. And making feeding the animals and collecting the eggs much easier.

THE MYSTERY OF
THE DEAD CHICKS

A true story that Veneta's sister Georgie passed on to Dale

Everyone was busy that day on the farm. Annie May was working in the house doing all the inside morning chores. Edgar, her oldest son, was out in the barn helping her Uncle Miller with barn tasks. Her daughter Veneta and son Bill were at school. Georgie and the other children were just trying to keep out from underfoot.

When Annie May carried some scraps of food out to be mixed into the compost to be spread in the garden when they needed it, horror of horrors, she discovered all her new young chicks, only weeks old, lying dead on the ground by the compost pile.

"Oh no!" she cried out. "All my chicks, my little fluffy chicks, are dead!"

Georgie heard her mother and ran to see what had happened, and there were the twelve young chicks lying flat on their backs, their little chicken legs sticking up in the air.

"Momma, what happened to them? What will we do?"

"There's not much we can do now," her mother told her, lifting one of the soft little bodies up. "I don't know what killed them so it wouldn't be safe to cook them up for dinner. Poor little things, such a sad waste."

But then she thought of their soft down feathers. The down would make the new pillow she was sewing so much nicer if it were mixed in with the clipped feather tips she was using. So with Georgie helping to gather up the feathers as fast as her mother could pluck them, they soon had a nice little sack of feathers, and the dead chicks were tossed in the dump in back of the compost pile.

It was a sad day. Annie May couldn't get the mystery of the chicks out of her mind as she finished stuffing and sewing the pillow. Later, when she went out and down by the barn to put more scraps on the compost, she saw an amazing sight. There were the chicks peeking over the top of the compost pile, just their heads at first with a few straggly feathers sticking up on top. Then one by one they came wobbling over the pile and down the slope, twelve funny looking naked chicks.

Annie May called everyone to come and see, even ran into the barn to get Edgar. He had been working hard with Annie May's Uncle Miller to make up her uncle's famous brew. And that solved the mystery of the naked chicks. They must have eaten some of the discarded mash that had been used to make the brew. Edgar admitted he had tossed it in the compost. The chickens hadn't been dead when Annie May had found and plucked them, they had been dead drunk.

When they woke up they must have been sore, and amazed that they were featherless and almost too dizzy to walk. And they must have also been startled by the family gathering around them, and all the laughter which did continue for a long time even after their feathers did eventually grow back.

ADDITIONAL DESCENDANTS

A place to add your own names and photographs